What's the Issue?

WHAT ARE GMOS?

By Simon Pierce

KidHaven
PUBLISHING

Published in 2024 by
KidHaven Publishing, an Imprint of Greenhaven Publishing, LLC
2544 Clinton Street
Buffalo, NY 14224

Designer: Deanna Paternostro
Editor: Jennifer Lombardo

Photo credits: Cover (top) Svetolia/Shutterstock.com; cover (bottom) Alina Rosanova/Shutterstock.com; p. 5 (main) Tada Images/Shutterstock.com; p. 5 (inset) courtesy of the U.S. Department of Agriculture; p. 7 David Moreno Hernandez/Shutterstock.com; p. 9 Attasit saentep/Shutterstock.com; p. 11 grayjay/Shutterstock.com; p. 13 a katz/Shutterstock.com; p. 15 cherryyblossom/Shutterstock.com; p. 17 bogdanhoda/Shutterstock.com; p. 19 itakdalee/Shutterstock.com; p. 21 Curly Pat/Shutterstock.com.

Cataloging-in-Publication Data

Names: Pierce, Simon.
Title: What are GMOs? / Simon Pierce.
Description: Buffalo, New York : KidHaven Publishing, 2024. | Series: What's the issue?| Includes glossary and index.
Identifiers: ISBN 9781534544086 (pbk.) | ISBN 9781534544093 (library bound) | ISBN 9781534544109 (ebook)
Subjects: LCSH: Transgenic organisms–Juvenile literature. | Crops–Genetic engineering–Juvenile literature. | Agricultural biotechnology–Juvenile literature.
Classification: LCC QH442.6 P54 2024 | DDC 338.1'7–dc23

Printed in the United States of America

CPSIA compliance information: Batch #CSKH24: For further information contact Greenhaven Publishing LLC at 1-844-317-7404.

Please visit our website, www.greenhavenpublishing.com. For a free color catalog of all our high-quality books, call toll free 1-844-317-7404 or fax 1-844-317-7405.

Find us on

CONTENTS

The Science of Genetics

When you look at the food on shelves in the grocery store, you might see two kinds of labels. One says "Bioengineered," and the other says "Non-GMO." What do these labels mean?

Every living thing has genes in it. Genes hold the information that control what traits a plant, animal, or person has. For example, the genes in corn tell it to grow tall and produce ears with yellow kernels, or seeds, on the inside and a green **husk** on the outside. Bioengineering is when people change the genes in something. We call that thing a genetically modified, or changed, organism—a GMO.

Facing the Facts

In 2020, 94 percent of soybeans, 96 percent of cotton, and 92 percent of corn planted in the United States were genetically modified (GM).

Shoppers can look for these pictures on food packaging to help them decide what to buy.

5% MILKFAT

GRADE A

Keeping Living Things Safe

Why would people bioengineer food? The main reason today is to help plants **resist** bugs, germs, or mold. The more plants survive, or keep living, the more food there is for people.

GMOs can also help keep people and animals healthy. If farmers don't have to spray **chemicals** on their plants to keep them alive because they're using bioengineering, the farmers won't breathe in those chemicals. Animals that are fed GM crops and people who buy those crops at the store won't eat those chemicals either.

Facing the Facts

In the mid-1800s, mold killed most of the potatoes in Ireland. Since potatoes were a big part of poor Irish people's diet, many people died. GMOs that resist mold could help stop this from happening again.

People have to cover up to stay safe
when they spray pesticides, or bug killers, on plants.

Helping the Environment

Another reason why people grow GMOs is because they can help the environment, or the natural world. Growing GM crops that are resistant to herbicides, or weed killers, lets farmers spray their crops with herbicides to control weeds without killing the crops. Spraying means they don't have to **till** the ground to control weeds. Untilled soil is healthier, so it can be easier for crops to grow in it.

Tilling the ground takes a lot of work from gas-powered machines. If farmers don't till, they put less carbon dioxide into the air. This is a gas that traps heat in the **atmosphere**, making Earth warmer.

Facing the Facts

Animals can be GMOs too. A type of salmon called the AquAdvantage salmon has been genetically modified so it grows faster and is ready to catch and eat sooner than other salmon.

Too much tilling can make it easy for wind and rain to erode, or wear away, the soil.

Is It Safe?

Some people don't like GMOs. They worry that changing a plant or animal's genes could make it less **nutritious** or make people sick if they eat it. However, scientists agree that these things aren't happening. A lot of studies have been done to make sure GMOs are safe and healthy for people and animals. If they made people sick, we'd know it by now!

Sometimes plants are bioengineered to be even more nutritious. For example, golden rice has been genetically modified to have vitamin A in it. In places where people have a hard time getting enough vitamin A, this rice could help provide it.

Facing the Facts 🔍

Farmers have been bioengineering crops for thousands of years. Corn has been changed so much from its wild form that it would not survive if humans stopped farming it.

10

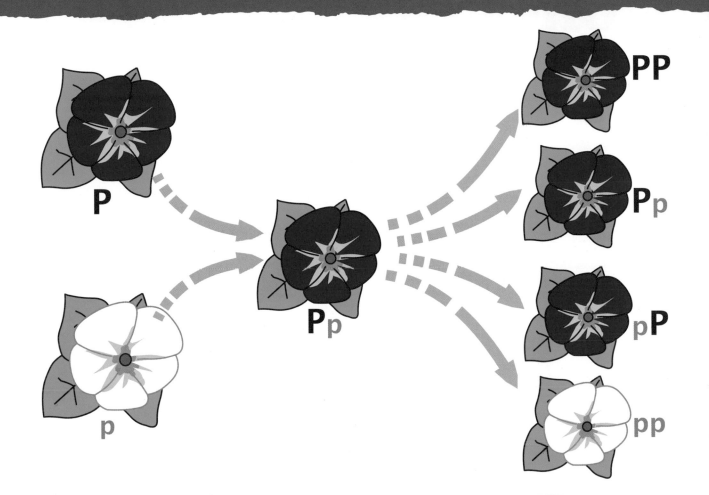

In 1865, Gregor Mendel—a monk and a **biologist**—shared his studies on plant genetics. This picture shows some of how it works. If a flower has even one capital P gene, it has red petals. The flower can only have white petals if it has two lowercase p genes and no capital P genes. We call the capital gene "dominant" and the lowercase gene "recessive." Genes come from our parents.

11

Concerns About Control

Another reason why people don't like GMOs is because they don't trust the companies that do the bioengineering. The companies create GM seeds and sell them to farmers. People tell stories about farmers getting in trouble when the wind blows some of those seeds into their fields and they grow by accident. Companies do **sue** farmers who use their seeds on purpose without paying. However, there hasn't been even one case where that happened accidentally.

Many people say farmers should be allowed to save the seeds from their crops and regrow them the next year. However, many farmers say they don't want to do that!

Facing the Facts

Many farmers don't save their seeds to replant because it's often cheaper and easier to buy new seeds every year. New seeds are also more likely to grow the way the farmer wants them to.

Monsanto used to be the largest GMO company until Bayer bought it.
Many people distrusted Monsanto and still distrust Bayer.

Concerns About Biodiversity

Another thing people worry about when it comes to GMOs is biodiversity. This is when the plants and animals in an area are different from each other. In farming, biodiversity is important because plants with different genes can withstand different things.

For example, if a farmer grows a soybean crop in which all the plants are genetically the same because they come from GM seeds, the whole crop can be wiped out at once by a sickness or bugs. However, if the plants are genetically diverse, some might be able to resist that disease or bug and will survive.

Facing the Facts 🔍

GMOs can be good or bad for biodiversity, depending on the location and crop. Farmers have to be careful when they plant GM seeds and think about all the things that could happen.

Plant biodiversity also helps **pollinators** such as bees and butterflies.

Laws About GMOs

Governments around the world have made laws about GMOs. Some countries say nothing is allowed to be bioengineered—even food for animals or crops that aren't going to be eaten at all! Some people worry that when farm animals eat GM plants, humans who eat the meat that comes from those animals will get sick. However, there's no scientific reason to think this is true.

In the United States, GMOs have been tested to make sure they're safe. The government also says bioengineered foods must be labeled so people can avoid them if they want to.

Facing the Facts 🔍

A living thing's genes don't change because of what it eats. If they did, you would be part cow after eating a hamburger or drinking a glass of milk!

Some people worry about GMOs being fed to animals. However, scientific studies have shown that nothing bad happens to animals that eat them.

Using Common Sense

There are a lot of people who think GMOs are great. There are also a lot of people who think GMOs are terrible. The truth is somewhere in between. GMOs can have problems, but they can also have a lot of **benefits**.

When you come across information about GMOs, it's important to take a look at where that information is coming from and whether it's backed up by science. For example, a company that sells "all-natural" items may write scary but untrue things about GMOs in its ads to make people more likely to buy its products.

Facing the Facts

It's good to question new science! By asking questions and **identifying** problems, scientists can keep making things better. It's also important to know when to believe in the results of science experiments.

18

Some beauty products,
such as moisturizer
or shampoo,
have **GMOs** in them.

How to Help

One of the best things you can do when it comes to GMOs is learn! Read more about what they are, how they're created, and what problems they might cause. Think about how those problems could be solved. When you hear people spread false information about GMOs, politely correct them.

Remember that people are often worried about new **technology**, including GMOs. Understanding the science behind the technology can often make people feel less worried. If you still feel concerned about GMOs, think about why you feel this way. What would you need to hear to make you feel better?

Facing the Facts 🔍

GMOs have to go through a lot of testing before they're allowed to be sold.

WHAT CAN YOU DO?

Talk to a farmer or biologist about GMOs.

Politely correct false information when you hear it.

Make a list of good and bad things about GMOs and how the bad things could be fixed.

Read more about GMOs.

Write to government leaders if you have strong feelings about GMO laws.

Learning more is the best thing you can do to help yourself and others understand GMOs.

GLOSSARY

atmosphere: The thick layer of gases that surrounds Earth.

benefit: A good or helpful result or effect.

biologist: A person who studies biology, or the branch of science that deals with living things.

chemical: Any substance that is formed when two or more other substances act upon one another or that is used to produce a change in another substance.

husk: The outer covering of a fruit or seed.

identify: To find out or show the identity of something or someone.

nutritious: Providing nutrients such as vitamins and minerals.

pollinator: An insect that fertilizes plants by bringing pollen from one plant to another.

resist: To withstand the force or effect of something.

sue: To bring a lawsuit against someone or something.

technology: The use of science in solving problems.

till: In farming, to dig up the ground to get rid of weeds or get the soil ready for crops.

FOR MORE INFORMATION

WEBSITES

Easy Science for Kids: GMOs
easyscienceforkids.com/gmos
Read more about the good and bad of GMOs.

YouTube: "What Is a Genetically Modified Food?"
www.youtube.com/watch?v=JMPE5wlB3Zk
Learn more about how scientists create GMOs.

BOOKS

Gregory, Josh. *Why We Need Plants*. New York, NY: Children's Press, 2020.

Loh-Hagan, Virginia. *Weird Science: Food*. Ann Arbor, MI: Cherry Lake Publishing, 2021.

Salt, Zelda. *Be a Geneticist*. New York, NY: Gareth Stevens Publishing, 2019.

INDEX